THE AXIS SATELLITES

AND

GREECE, OUR ALLY

By

CLARENCE A. MANNING

Acting Executive Officer
Department of East European Languages
Columbia University

▼

ANATOLIA PRESS — NEW YORK

1946

Printed in U. S. A.

CONTENTS

INTRODUCTION

It is one of the tragedies of a great war that people are so relieved at its successful conclusion that they show an all too great unwillingness to think seriously and to act firmly to carry out all the goals which they had set for themselves at the beginning of the struggle. That unity and resolution, that assurance that victory must be complete which had animated the people during the struggle, disappears rapidly and they are replaced by an impatience for the restoration of so-called normal conditions and a tendency to ignore many questions which were of the most direct concern but a short time before. This is especially the case when the question arises of assisting the various small nations which have taken part in the struggle and which must look to their more powerful allies for understanding and justice.

It was true in 1918 when there came a curious mixture of idealism and of power politics which declined to settle all the problems of Europe. It is perhaps more true of the situation of 1946. The terrible character of the war, the discovery of new weapons and of the atom bomb have so aroused a wave of public sentiment that men and women are talking only of world organization and of means of preventing another holocaust that might destroy civilization. They often cannot see that a world organization can only be useful if it is founded on the principles of justice and humanity and that the most pressing task is to give a just answer to the crying evils that had so much to do with the precipitation of the last war. They often forget that millions of lives have been wasted in vain, if the victors are going to neglect the principles for which they fought and to rest content with a meaningless idealism which refuses to face facts.

It is this failure to undertake the responsibility of correcting the situation and this willingness to rest content with idealistic platitudes that create the discords of the future. The omissions and the errors of 1918 created the situation that exploded in 1939 and made mockery of all the hopes of mankind. The failure now to take decisive action can likewise but sow the seeds and arm the passions for the next war and there can be little doubt that every day the present indifference is allowed to develop it is only strengthening the forces of disintegration of human society and rendering more impotent the true idealistic hopes of humanity.

The world does not willingly look back after the ending of the struggle to consider the hopes and aspirations with which it entered it. It all too obligingly forgets its judgments of but a few years before and regards as nuisances those people who try to revive the past.

Greece is a case in point. In 1940 and 1941, the entire democratic world was applauding her heroic defense against the armies of Fascist Italy and of Nazi Germany when she by her sheer valor defeated Italy and delayed the German attack on the Soviet Union. The newspapers were filled with tributes to the bravery of the Greek soldiers, the exploits of the evzones, and the self-sacrificing aid given to the Allies by the Greek navy and fishermen. Everyone recognized that Greece well deserved the recovery of the Dodecanesian Islands, that she well merited protection against the repeated and continuous aggressions of Bulgaria which had attacked her three times in thirty years, that she should have protection against Italy and Albania which had been the puppet of Italy, etc., etc.

To-day with peace at hand, public sentiment is so concentrated on winning the good will of the Soviet Union and in satisfying that country's ambitions for the Slavic states of the Balkans that it pays no attention to the plight of Greece. It forgets willingly all that the Greeks have done for victory at the cost of a million lives and many billions of property and it all too often tacitly repudiates its obligation of helping Greece to achieve those legitimate goals which alone can restore the country to prosperity and allow her to develop as a peaceful member of a new and better world. It pays no attention to the recrudescence of those unfortunate tendencies that created the debacle of 1939 and which are already in much the same form daring again to advance the old theories and claims.

No amount of clever sophistry, no juggling with the meaning of words as "democracy," no legal technicalities can conceal the fact that the high hopes cherished in the dark days of the war, that were embodied in the Atlantic Charter and the Four Freedoms, are being systematically set aside. The idealists and men of good will are so concentrating on the hope of a world organization to promote permanent peace that they ignore those happenings which are already nullifying their desires and paralyzing statesmen who are trying to overcome them and the cynics and the aggressors are thus given a chance to do their deadly work.

Let us then look at the relations of Greece with her neighbors and see what she can expect from them in the future.

ITALY

The rise of Benito Mussolini and of Fascism are often taken by the people of the Allied countries to mark the turn of Italian policy from one of peace to one of aggression. Events have moved so swiftly in the past half century that the convulsions of the early years have been thrown into obscurity by the later and more overwhelming events. The world cannot appreciate that it must look back to the years before the First War to judge the policy and the motives of many of the men who have emerged from long obscurity to become now prominent in the new Italy after the disastrous failure of Fascism.

Fascism owed one of its great sources of strength to the widespread belief that modern Italy was destined to revive the Roman Empire. Had that not existed, the antics of Mussolini would have aroused only passing interest and would not have swept the various classes of the population into its all-embracing arms. The same harbors and mountain valleys still exist as in the past. The same impulses continue and it is not without significance that an Italy determined to expand should follow very largely the same path that Rome had marked out almost two thousand years ago.

From the moment when Italy became a united nation after 1870, the Italian statesmen sought for some way to become a world power. Before the time of Christ, Italy had plundered Greece and had brought its rich artistic treasures in large numbers to Rome. The Fourth Crusade which shamelessly plundered Constantinople in the thirteenth century and created the final emotional barriers to a satisfactory solution of the difficulties between the Roman Catholic and the Orthodox Churches was engineered by the Venitians who profited again by bringing Greek works of art to that city. The Greeks cannot forget that it was the Venitians who destroyed the Parthenon in 1687. The Italian city states as each grew powerful sought expansion in the Balkans and it was Greece that was perpetually attacked.

With a united Italy, the question of the Adriatic Sea at once became all prominent and next to that the Mediterranean. Italy's advance along the north shore of Africa, Tripoli and the Cyrenaica, were all part of a deliberate policy to turn the Mediterranean Sea into an Italian lake. It was this policy, steadily becoming more vocal and more definite, that inspired Italy to undertake the Italian-Turkish War of 1911 and brought her the Dodecanesus, entirely inhabited by Greeks. The occupation of Rhodes was hailed as an Italian victory, even though there was scarcely any fighting between the Italians and the Turks.

Then came the long and tragic story of the Italian occupation of the islands and the atrocities of long years against the Greek population. Italy may have played with the idea of restoring their liberty but by the time that the First World War broke out, Italy demanded recognition of her sovereignty over them and was promised it in the Secret Treaty of London of April 26, 1915. The people of the Dodecanesus were not consulted. They protested again and again and on Easter Day, 1919, while the Peace Conference was in session in Paris, Italian troops attacked the people of Rhodes for daring to send a delegation to the Conference to ask reunion with their mother country.

For a moment it seemed as if Italy might be influenced to pay some attention to the ideals of democracy and self-determination that had been outlined by President Wilson, but only for a moment. On July 29, 1919, Signor Tittoni as Minister of Foreign Affairs signed an accord with Mr. Venizelos to restore all the Dodecanesus except Rhodes to Greece and, if England restored Cyprus, to allow a plebiscite in Rhodes. Another clause provided that Greece would receive in recompense Northern Epirus which forms the southern part of Albania. It was only a blind, for within a year, that democrat, Count Sforza, now President of the Italian Assembly, denounced the agreement and Italy, by the agreements with Turkey, secured control of the Dodecanesus with the approval of the Allied nations who hoped thus to prevent a second World War and to promote harmony at the expense of justice and right.

Thus it was democratic Italy that laid the basis for the development of the new Roman Empire in the eastern Mediterranean. Count Sforza and the democrats of 1918 laid the groundwork for the aggressions of Mussolini and the Fascists. Had the Peace Conference and the President of the United States listened to the serious resolutions of the United States Senate passed in 1920, for the award of the Dodecanesian Islands and Northern Epirus to the Kingdom of Greece, the way would have been paved for the saving of thousands of lives in 1941. But peace was in the air and Greece was the small country selected to suffer.

The same was true in even greater detail with the province of Northern Epirus. Under the agreements between the Balkan states in the First Balkan War, the territory was awarded to Greece and was liberated by the Greek armies. This was too much for Italy to tolerate and there began the intrigues which resulted in the attack by Bulgaria on her former Allies in 1913. Unfortunately for Italy and Austria-Hungary, Bulgaria was defeated and it was necessary for the intriguing powers to take matters into their own hands and at the Council of Florence at the end of the year, the Triple Alliance of Germany, Austria-Hungary and Italy succeeded in bluffing England and France into agreeing to the inclusion of the territory into Albania.

During the spring of 1914 when Prince William of Wied was in control of Albania and remained on a foreign warship in the harbor of Durazzo, there came an uprising for liberty by the Greeks in the province and the European powers were compelled by the force of circumstances to recognize the province as autonomous and to give rights to the Greek population. This was followed during the period of the First World War before Italy formally joined England and France by an occupation by Greek forces at the request of the democratic nations, but again at the end of the war, the secret treaties made to detach Italy from the Triple Alliance forced the Greeks to abandon the province, which was turned over to Albania.

Thus the basis for Italian policy was laid long before the rise of Mussolini and the guilt of the Fascists lay rather in the pushing of the imperialist policy laid down by the democratic statesmen of Italy rather than in the inauguration of something new and definite by Fascist Italy. There was only a greater emphasis and a greater efficiency in advancing her schemes against Greece and the policy shifted only from planning to win over unorganized tribes to effecting a definite control over an Albania which as a member of the League of Nations was supposed to have an independent vote in the gatherings of the civilized peoples of the world.

The methods employed by the Italian government in Albania were simple. It was merely to lend so much money to the young Albanian state that it could never hope to pay off its obligations and obtain a free hand to manage its own affairs. This was done by one treaty after another. Costly bridges were built throughout the country, even when there were only miserable roads to approach them. Money was poured out like water to get the Albanian government into their clutches and after King Zogu himself fell for the bait by the Treaty of 1934, it was obvious that the country would soon be swallowed up.

This came in 1939 when under the double threat of Italian invasion and the revolt of Italian inspired tribesmen, King Zogu was forced to flee Albania. Then the country was duly annexed and Mussolini could look out at the world with more satisfaction than could the democratic statesmen of Italy in 1919 who had been unable to carry out all that they dreamed.

All that was left was for the Italians to carry out the next step in their traditional program. They had secured a firm base for the attack on Greece which their statesmen had planned for decades. They were able to concentrate their forces in their new domains on the east shore of the Adriatic and they hoped for nothing more.

All during the early part of 1940 the Italians were busy in making the necessary preparations and with the same guile that had covered their movements during the First World War, they attempted to lull to sleep the Greek people with a long series of announcements as to the community of interests between Italy and Greece. At the same time there began to appear sporadic instances of Italian bombing of Greek ships in Greek ports and finally the torpedoing of the Greek cruiser "Helli" in the harbor of Tinos on the Feast of the Assumption, August 15. Of course the Italians immediately denied this and tried to lay the blame on the British but investigation showed that the torpedoes bore the Italian trade mark.

Then a short time later came the final blow. The Italian troops that had been mobilized in Albania suddenly struck on October 28, 1940, and almost at once they were able to cross the Albanian border into Greece. They used again the traditional gateway into Greece from Northern Epirus and vindicated again the wisdom of the Greek government that had for two decades been endeavoring to persuade the democratic powers that this area was Greek and necessary to the security of Greece.

Events turned out contrary to expectation. The world was amazed when the Greeks with inferior forces rallied against the unexpected attack and threw the Italians back. In one battle after another the Greeks conquered. They liberated their own territory and then invaded the puppet state, now fully part of the Italian Empire. By the end of January, 1941, practically all of Northern Epirus, including the two Italian bases of Argyrokastro and

Korytsa, was in Greek hands. It was but a question of time when Valona would fall and the entire Italian position become intolerable. To save themselves, the Italians invoked the aid of Hitler and then with the aid of the Bulgarians, the Germans launched the overwhelming attack that carried them through Greece and added occupation and destruction to the plight of the gallant country which fought a two-front war that turned the tide in the favor of the Allies.

Time passed and the downfall of the Fascist policies before the advance of the United Nations put an end to Mussolini and his supporters. In their place there reappeared the older advocates of Italian imperialism. These men very graciously cancelled the annexation of Albania but they very soon began again to advance the arguments that Italy should be allowed some rights, commercial at least, in Albania. And of course Albania should control Northern Epirus.

It is the same argument as in 1919, with the subtle difference that this time it is the United Nations Organization instead of the old League. Policies can wait for fulfilment. The temporary rapid advance of Mussolini brought about its own destruction. The older diplomats can now revert to a slower and surer and less flamboyant policy but the only safe course will be to strengthen Greece and by restoring the territory that she should have, put her into a position where she can safely defend herself. Such a course is the only one to insure peace in the Balkans.

ALBANIA

Albania offers a peculiar problem to all those who are interested in Balkan peace and prosperity. It is a small state, the smallest of the area, and there are perhaps more Albanian-speaking persons outside of the country in Italy, Yugoslavia and Greece than there are in Albania proper. All the educated classes of these feel themselves more at home with their neighbors than they would among the tribesmen who form the bulk of the state.

There are scattered fragments of the Albanian language from the time of their national hero Skanderbeg in the fifteenth century but the national revival started among the Albanians in Italy and secondarily among those who had aroused the ill will of the Turkish government which severely suppressed attempts to develop an independent Albanian culture.

When the Albanian state was established, it was forced to draw almost exclusively upon the Italo-Albanians and a few anti-Turkish Albanians for such personnel as it required for the higher grades of its service. The very nature of the agitation for its creation increased their power, for Albania was from its inception intended to be a storm centre in the Balkans. Its wisest statesmen realized this but unfortunately most of them wished to profit by it and far too frequently put themselves at the disposal of trouble makers.

After the First World War, it was Italy that could afford to be the most liberal, for a chauvinistic Albanian policy fitted in with the plans of Italian foreign policy. Yet even so, the Italian policy was double edged, for what it built up and constructed, it in turn tore down. It had no desire to see a strong Albania which might win through the storms of tribal warfare and establish herself. The result was a constant struggle between Christians and Mohammedans, which reacted most strongly on Northern Epirus where the Greek element formed the best trained and best educated part of the population and was the numerical majority. In this area there took place a continuous series of atrocities to wipe out the Greek majority of the population and destroy their property and traditions. These attempts were intensified after the Albanians assisted the Italians in their invasion of Greece.

It is too much to hope that after six years of occupational and of Nazi and Fascist rule and misrule the old tendencies have been eliminated. All the evidence suggests that there has been a new shift of emphasis and the reports of the elections that gave eighty five per cent of the vote for the one party ticket raises again the question of the real meaning of democracy in the country. The feuds between the leaders of the various anti-Nazi bands and the quarrels abroad bear witness to the same situation. It is all too evident that passions are still running high and that those forces which are still working to keep the Balkans from entering upon a peaceful existence are in control.

During two World Wars, Albania was a battleground in which the various tribes took part according to their own interest and their own hates and feuds. There was no central spokesman and even the deposed King made but a half-hearted attempt to assert his rights and speak for his people. None of his ministers came out strongly and openly against the Italian occupation. It was the conscience of the democratic nations, rather, that impelled them to refuse to recognize the annexation by Italy and the new government is but a backwash of events in the Balkans.

There has long been fostered a deliberate anti-Greek feeling quite unlike the attitude toward the Yugoslavs. It was deliberately inflamed by Italy and now is flourishing with the backing of the new Slav movement which is supported by the Soviet Union in one form or another. The hostility of that movement to Greece and the Greeks has long been recognized and it is constantly growing stronger.

It is the task of the Albanian leaders to check this anti-Greek feeling and bring about a real rapprochement but until this is done, it is folly to jeopardize peace by giving the Albanian government control of Northern Epirus and full mastery of the ports that control the entrance to northern Greece and the heart of the Balkans. Rather Albania needs more than any other country disinterested economic and educational aid so that the people can be prepared to play their part in the new world.

The history of Northern Epirus since 1913 has shown a constant alternation between the great democratic powers and the various aggressor nations. The former have consistently assigned it to Greece, the latter to Albania and the threat of war has been raised consistently in all international conferences to aid the latter. It is curious that now there should be any hesitation in opposing the policies so well developed and supported by Italian imperialism.

BULGARIA

The three attacks on Greece by Bulgaria during the last thirty years are themselves symptoms of a deep seated dream of the Bulgarian people. The revival of the Bulgarian national consciousness at the end of the eighteenth century was inspired by a desire to restore the First Bulgarian Empire which extended its control over most of the Balkans for a short period of years in the tenth century.

That desire was revived by the Russian diplomats at the Treaty of San Stefano in 1876 and it has been the dream of every Bulgarian statesman. It was present in the minds of King Ferdinand and his counsellors when they started the Second Balkan War. It was present again when the same people treacherously attacked Greece and Serbia in 1915 to please the Germans in the First World War. The government was forced into exile but during the turbulent period that followed, there was no government that would dare to defy this mood of the people.

Under such conditions, the marriage of King Boris to an Italian princess could not fail to bring the Bulgarian foreign policy into close connection with that of Italy and later with that of Germany. Irredentism became the main element of Bulgarian thought and it could only poison all attempts to restore normal conditions within the peninsula.

When Germany attacked Greece in 1941, it seemed a golden opportunity for Bulgaria, which had already profited by the territorial decisions of der Führer, to join in the war and secure again the territory which she desired. She marched at once into Greece and immediately began to exterminate the Greek population without regard to any feelings of humanity or justice. Atrocities were the order of the day. Any pro-American and pro-democratic elements in Bulgaria sank into silence and the people rallied to the cause of the government as it declared war upon the United States.

When it became certain, that the Fascist powers could not win, the mood changed and there came a revolution. The so-called Fascist leaders were liquidated along with any who had shown signs of friendliness to Greece and a new Communist-oriented government came into power. It was no real reform, for the old ideas still persisted. Archbishop Stefan, formerly head of the Society of Father Paisi, one of the most bitter irredentist groups, became the formal head of the church.

The Bulgarian Academy of Sciences, purged of its Fascist imperialistic members, continues to pour out even in 1945 and 1946 the same violent demands for a return of the shore of the Aegean Sea and Salonika and openly says that Balkan peace and prosperity hinges upon the granting to Bulgaria of all those goals for which she went into war on the side of the Fascists, fought the democratic powers including the United States, and for which she destroyed cruelly so many thousands of Greeks.

It is one of the tragic outcomes of the Second World War that there has been no modification of the attitudes which caused that war. Understanding seems more remote than six years ago. The death of kings and diplomats and professors has meant little to the neighbors of Greece and the first steps of peace and reconciliation have yet to be laid.

Bulgaria is a case at point. All indications show that even in defeat and revolution, she has not abandoned any of her ambitious plans and we can understand the anxiety of the Greeks as they see the renewed evidences of international support for the nation which has so often attacked her treacherously and sided with Germany in the two World Wars.

CONCLUSION

Greece to-day is in an unhappy situation. Political events since the liberation have served to dim the glory of her resistance against overwhelming odds to the Fascist and Nazi forces that attacked her. The newspapers of the world have been filled with stories of discord and civil strife. The position of Greece is contrasted with those of the neighboring countries where elections go through automatically with tremendous majorities for the party in power which in every case is Communist-dominated.

The world knows of the Greek chaos. It is not allowed to learn so easily of the technique that is being applied in the Slavonic countries where a strong man with the backing of the Soviet Union and the Pan-Slav organization of Moscow can ride roughshod over an entire population. It does not understand that the tradition of Greece is one with the Western countries and that the tradition is so interwoven with the Greek spirit that civilization which sprang from it can still depend upon it.

Greece is now and always has been connected with the sea. Her aid to the Allies in north Africa and on the seven seas and in the defense of her homeland was tied up with the courage and skill of her sailors no less than of her heroic soldiers and airmen. Her people are largely islanders.

What then are the needs of Greece in the post-war world? She needs again a practicable land frontier which can easily be given her without intruding on the claims of peaceful neighbors. She needs the Greek islands and it is rank hypocrisy to suggest that the return of the Dodecanesus must be held up in order to make them outposts of the Soviet position on the Dardanelles or examples of universal trusteeship in some form or another. She needs a modification of the Greek-Bulgarian frontier for reasons of her safety. She needs reparations from Italy, Germany, Bulgaria, and Albania, the nations which slaughtered her population and devastated her country, so that she can recover her former prosperity and play her part in the world of the future.

The experience of the nations at the end of the Napoleonic Wars and at the end of the First World War have proved that peacemaking is no complicated thing, if the leaders appear with clean hands and pure hearts. It becomes frightfully complicated when one or more of the Great Powers are endeavoring to expand materially or ideologically. The war for democracy, as this word has been understood for centuries, has been won. The peace is being daily more confused, as idealists and lovers of humanity plan a world organization and refuse to see that justice and human rights are an inalienable part of it.

Had Greece received her due in 1919, she would have played a still more effective part in 1940. We can only hope that the democratic powers will not yield again but will declare openly that she is to have Northern Epirus and Dodecanesus and have them now. Then undoubtedly when peace is definitely made, Cyprus with its long tradition of Greek civilization and its overwhelming Greek population will undoubtedly find her place in the restored Greece. More than any other nation, Greece stood out in the dark days of the struggle. It is only right that the Great Powers should recognize her merits, undo the work of countless intrigues, and grant her what she well deserves.

Date Due